Living with Illness and Suffering

The Catholic way to hope and healing

by
Rev Nick Donnelly

*All booklets are published thanks to the
generous support of the members of the
Catholic Truth Society*

CATHOLIC TRUTH SOCIETY
PUBLISHERS TO THE HOLY SEE

Contents

To my mother and father, with love and thanks

All rights reserved. First published 2010 by The Incorporated Catholic Truth Society, 40-46 Harleyford Road, London SE11 5AY Tel: 020 7640 0042 Fax: 020 7640 0046. Copyright © 2010 The Incorporated Catholic Truth Society.

ISBN 978 1 86082 664 1

Purpose of this booklet

This book of prayers, practical advice, meditations, and reflections has been written for people coping with suffering caused by chronic conditions such as long-term sickness, disability, grief, depression, anxiety, and many other afflictions.

I became ill in 1987, and was soon housebound and unable to work. It took 5 years for the doctors to diagnose a chronic, incurable sickness, plus other complications. It took another 5 years for them to get it under reasonable control. I remain in permanent poor health subject to severe pain, susceptible to infections and with a higher risk of developing cancer.

The inspiration for this book was an event that happened almost 12 years ago. I was undergoing a flare up of the disease, and was lying on the bathroom floor, unable to move due to severe abdominal pain. I must admit that I was frightened and this fear was making the pain worse.

In my anxiety I asked Martina, my wife, to bring me a crucifix that I gripped hard with each spasm of pain. Instead of focusing on the pain I focused on Jesus' sufferings on the Cross. It was as if, lying on the floor, I joined my pain with his pain on Calvary, and my fear subsided. After a while, the pain lessened enough for Martina to help me back to bed.

By an act of grace, I had learnt the truth of St Peter's words, 'through his wounds you have been healed' (1 *Peter* 2:24). By this, I don't mean that miraculously my disease had gone, but that Christ's wounds began to transform my experience of suffering.

I have found that devotion to the wounds of Christ has given meaning and purpose to my trials, which in turn has blessed me with enough perseverance and hope to build a life that is much more than suffering. A life brightened by joy and consolations even when I am in pain.

At a time when a vocal minority are pushing assisted suicide onto the sick and disabled as the only way of escaping our suffering, we must make more widely known the Catholic understanding of the dignity, value and transformational power of suffering shared with the Crucified God.

It is my hope that others who are trying to cope with suffering, in all its aspects, will find some help here.

Deacon Nick Donnelly
St Mary of Furness, Barrow,
Diocese of Lancaster, Lent 2010

The impact of suffering

'Like water I am poured out, disjointed are all my bones. My heart has become like wax, it is melted within my breast. Parched as burnt clay is my throat, my tongue cleaves to my jaw. You lay me down in the dust of death'. (*Psalm* 22:14-15).

Suffering comes to us all, at some time in our lives, as the poet Henry Longfellow puts it, 'Into each life some rain must fall, some days must be dark and dreary.'

But for some suffering is like a daily, relentless deluge that soaks every part of their lives, getting everywhere. For others, it is more like a devastating hurricane that uproots everything, forever changing the landscape of their lives. For yet others they have to endure both catastrophic suffering and chronic suffering.

Chronic suffering includes all types of chronic health conditions caused by physical diseases, genetic preconditions, accidents, disabilities, addictions, and mental health conditions, such as bipolar disorder, depression, neuroses and phobias. Chronic means 'long-term'.

My chronic sickness has left no aspect of my life untouched, including relationships, work, leisure activities, prayer and sacramental life, even things as basic as diet and sleep.

Suffering isolates

Some of the hardest things to cope with in suffering any chronic condition are the long periods of isolation from normal life caused by being housebound. It feels like the world carries on, while your own life grinds to a halt. When I'm unable to work or enjoy the ordinary pleasures of life, my world often shrinks to the size of my home, sometimes just to my bedroom and bathroom.

Without the stimulation of working relationships, going to church, or the essential exchanges of friendship, it is so easy to feel cut off from life.

Also, feeling constantly unwell and in pain quite naturally forces your attention inwards, where all kinds of resentments, fears and doubts can too easily dominate your thoughts.

Furthermore, in my experience most healthy people don't understand what it really means to live with a chronic disease or condition. At first, when you become sick, people are considerate and solicitous, but as the months pass with no improvement, many stop calling. Not only is chronic suffering boring, it also reminds others of the mortality and pain of life, which most people, not surprisingly, want to avoid.

I have also found that there are judgmental and critical attitudes towards chronic conditions that add to the sense of isolation. We live in a society in which many increasingly make the mistake of judging quality of life strictly in terms of independence of action, unrestricted freedom of choice, physically active life-styles and youthful looks.

Sadly, it is becoming all too common to encounter impatience, even intolerance, towards any form of dependence, limitation, disability or sign of old age. This is just one expression of the contemporary denial of the inevitability of suffering, ageing and death.

It is all too easy for those of us suffering chronic conditions to succumb to the pressure of these opinions and feel we're failures and outsiders, and in the worst cases, burdens on society.

Over the years I've gradually come to appreciate being an outsider. Being an outsider through learning to live with suffering and my own mortality has helped me focus on questions of ultimate concern, instead of being caught up in the rush of modern life.

The sick room, like the desert, can be a harsh place where life is stripped down to its essentials. In my experience chronic suffering presents us with the fundamental decision of existence - either to trust God to guide us through life or to reject God's plan for our lives by blaming him for our condition and cursing life as meaningless and pointless. Chronic suffering reveals the heart of man, bringing out the best or the worst in us.

'Illness can lead to anguish, self-absorption, sometimes even despair and revolt against God. It can also make a person more mature, helping him discern in his life what is not essential so that he can turn toward that which is. Very often illness provokes a search for God and a return to him'. (CCC, 1501).

Suffering frustrates

Most people's sense of personal identity and their place in society derives from their work. This is reflected in the fact that in conversation people often ask, 'What do you do?' or 'How's work going?'

There have been times when I have dreaded these questions, because it is so frustrating to have to reply, 'I'm not able to work due to illness'.

One of the hardest things I've found about being chronically ill is enforced inactivity due to pain, lack of energy or some other disabling symptom.

Most of us grow up with a vision of how we'd like our lives to unfold; some even have definite plans for a career, marriage and a family. We want our lives to mean something, to make a difference, but instead, due to our chronic condition, we find ourselves imprisoned by our bodies or minds!

There have been times when I've hated my body for being beyond my control, because no matter how much I want to do something, if I'm sick or in pain I just can't go outside when I want to, or go to work, or visit friends or family, or go to important events like marriages, baptisms or funerals. It can be frustrating beyond words!

One of the worst things about chronic suffering can be the feeling of not being in control and life not making any sense. There's a saying, 'Nature abhors a vacuum', and this applies in a specific way to chronic suffering. Faced with the lack of control and meaninglessness we try to force control and meaning onto our lives. But often this is a negative type of control and meaning - blaming ourselves, our doctors, or even God.

This negative attitude can begin a very destructive downward spiral, because blame tends to transform all our frustrated and imprisoned energy into recrimination, rage and bitterness. Like all emotions, these violent feelings seek to express themselves either through self-criticism or self-hate or through lashing out at those around us, usually those closest to us.

Living with a chronic condition can be hard but when such negative thoughts also become dominant, life can become absolutely intolerable for others and ourselves.

It's not surprising that some seek relief from their desperate situation through alcohol, drugs or pornography. However, these only provide an illusory escape, and make matters worse through increasing the sense of being out of control and the meaninglessness of life. They also harm a body and psyche already weak and vulnerable.

After years of coping with a chronic health condition, I've learnt that the best approach is to try to live within the constraints imposed by the disease.

This means being aware of what you can do and what you can't do, and realising that you only have a limited amount of energy to expend on work or other activities.

It is important to try to take enough rest before and after doing things to avoid a relapse. However, sometimes I find it difficult to live by this rule because my enthusiasm to do things makes me throw caution to the wind, even if unwise.

The other way of coping with a chronic condition is through learning to adapt to the situation by trying to transform restrictions into opportunities. For example, I have taken advantage of the time and solitude to deepen my knowledge and understanding of the Faith, and myself. I have developed ways of expressing my insights through sculpture and writing which have brought new meaning and direction.

However, there are times when I've be in so much pain or feeling so unwell that I haven't got the energy or wellbeing to do anything but lie in bed and wait untill things improve.

When I've been in constant pain or have been feeling unwell for months I've had no choice but to retreat to the safety of my home to rest and let my body recover. However, one of the problems associated with chronic conditions can be an understandable reluctance to go back out into the rough and tumble of the world. Without even noticing, our home can change from being our refuge to our prison.

It was only when I realised that I couldn't help myself and I needed someone to rescue me from the prison of my body, that the truth of Jesus being my Saviour became real for me. It was only when I was at the end of my strength and in desperate need that I heard these words as if for the first time.

It is truly liberating to realise that the course of our lives does not depend solely on physical strength, health and will-power but on our willingness to trust the Holy Spirit to open up new possibilities and guide us along the right path.

Don't misunderstand me. When I'm in great pain or feel very sick, I often find it difficult to trust God, when all I can do is hold on to my faith by my fingertips. But I know, deep down, that such trust is the only way to cope with chronic suffering.

This means gradually becoming sensitive to the promptings and guidance of the Holy Spirit through regular prayer, the sacraments and reflection on Scripture.

Suffering humiliates

Other hard things to cope with during a chronic illness are the times when we lose our sense of personal dignity and self-esteem. For example, the disease may have embarrassing symptoms or entail embarrassing medical examinations. I have not found this easy, but accepting that this has become a permanent part of my life has helped me to adapt and become less sensitive than I was in the early years.

It can also be humiliating to have to reveal intimate aspects about our lives over and over to doctors and nurses who, through no fault of their own, can seem impersonal and detached.

Having said this, I have been treated with great respect and thoughtfulness by some doctors and nurses, who have done everything they can to help me cope with my disease. Having a supportive and understanding GP and Consultant is essential to learning to live with a chronic condition. I have been fortunate in finding caring medical professionals, and they have made a great difference to my quality of life. If your GP or Consultant is not helpful consider whether you can transfer to the care of others.

The worst is when medical professionals treat patients as unfeeling objects; the best is when they relate to us as fellow human beings.

Another source of humiliation endured by people suffering chronic conditions occurs when they cannot work and must depend on insurance payments and social security benefits. Due to the prevalence of fraudulent claims, insurance companies and social services seem to start from the presumption of suspicion and doubt, which can be an unbearable source of stress to the genuinely sick.

It is profoundly humiliating when feeling very unwell and vulnerable to have one's integrity and truthfulness questioned by people whose overriding goal is to find a reason to stop your insurance payments or benefits.

Sadly, the most difficult type of humiliation to cope with, or get over, is loss of dignity as a result of the callousness, insensitivity or bullying from people we trust to care for us - a minority of medical and social service professionals.

It's a sad fact of life that some people enjoy exercising power in cruel and petty ways over others who are vulnerable and dependent. Equally they may act in an insensitive or intimidating way to cover up incompetence or mistakes.

In such situations it's not surprising that the sick find it difficult to complain because they are frightened or don't want to be branded as 'trouble-makers' when they are dependent on the care of others. Also, it is not uncommon for professions and institutions to close ranks to protect the offender and their reputation.

However, if the behaviour of the professional could be serious abuse, either physical or emotional, it is essential that you make an official complaint, with the support of your family and friends.

It's also important to ask for the grace to forgive those who betray our trust; otherwise we waste, in bitterness and anger, valuable energy needed for healing our minds and bodies.

Jesus with us

Everytime I look at the tortured figure of Jesus on the Crucifix I am reminded of this truth - when I experience 'the evil' of my illness or the evil of human beings, Jesus is here with me. In the promise of his presence, whether I feel it or not in his promise of victory over evil, and through his miracles (the greatest is his resurrection from the dead) Jesus is here with me.

When you know this truth, deep down, no suffering and no person can take away your dignity and self-esteem, no matter how humiliating the symptoms of your illness or the medical procedure or the behaviour of another person.

In fact, suffering forges a special bond between Jesus and us, - something we do not have when we are strong, healthy and self-reliant.

It is for these reasons that I have found meditating on the wounds and sufferings of Jesus such an important source of grace and meaning as I struggle to live with chronic illness. One thing I have learnt is that Christ's wounds transform our experience of suffering.

The dark side of chronic suffering

This combination of isolation, frustration, and humiliation over a prolonged period of time can lead to serious psychological and spiritual problems that can make matters worse.

One of the most difficult periods I have so far undergone was a period when I had no sense of God's presence, which left me feeling abandoned and unprotected. I also had to contend with unbidden thoughts that mocked my faith as a foolish illusion and the conviction that there was no heaven after death, only annihilation that would forever separate me from my loved ones. I began to dread trying to go to sleep at night, when these upsetting thoughts were strongest.

Through an act of will, I carried on my routine of daily prayer, and received the sacraments; I received no consolation, only abandonment and darkness. This went on for months. When I thought of giving up and rejecting my faith, these words of St Peter became my steadfast anchor:

So Jesus asked the twelve, "Do you also wish to go away?" Simon Peter answered him, "Lord, to whom can we go? You have the words of eternal life. We have come to believe and know that you are the Holy One of God." (*John* 6:67-68).

When I discussed this with a doctor he immediately interpreted my spiritual crisis as a reactive depression. Looking back, I'm still not certain if it was a form of depression, or a type of dark night (a recognised stage of the spiritual life) or a mixture of both!

Seeking help

However, the important thing to do when suffering mental and emotional anguish is to seek outside help. I undertook a short course of Cognitive Behavioural Therapy and saw a Spiritual Director for three years, when I was well enough. It all helped but, of course, had no effect on the underlying chronic illness.

It is essential that you exercise caution when seeking outside help because there are a great many people offering counselling, healing and alternative health remedies that either financially exploit the desperation of chronically sick people, or are unsympathetic and ignorant towards the Catholic faith, or are seeking power over others. Such people can do more harm than good.

If you suspect you are suffering a form of depression, it's best to seek advice from your GP and if you are struggling with a spiritual problem, talk to your parish priest who may, himself, be able to help you or recommend someone else with experience of the spiritual life.

Pope Benedict XVI recommends that everyone needs a spiritual director to help us gain deeper self-knowledge, deeper union with the Lord and mould our lives to the Gospel:

'To advance towards the Lord we always have need of a guide, of some form of dialogue; we cannot do it just with our own reflections. And finding this guide is part of the ecclesial nature of our faith'. (Pope Benedict XVI, Wednesday audience, 16th September 2009).

Temptation to suicide

One other dark side of chronic suffering is the temptation to commit suicide, out of despair and self-hate. Being in constant pain and feeling sick and unwell every day can leave us vulnerable to self-destructive thoughts.

Even some of the saints have been tempted by thoughts of suicide. When St Thérèse of Lisieux was suffering severe pain from terminal TB she admits she was tempted to kill herself on several occasions. She wrote, 'Oh, if I didn't have the Faith, I could never endure all this pain. I'm amazed that atheists don't commit suicide more often!'

Tragically, this temptation is being increasingly promoted as reasonable and humane in a utilitarian society that sees no value in patience and courage in the face of suffering. Not surprisingly, society's increasing intolerance towards the sick and dependent has lead a vocal minority to campaign for the legalisation of assisted suicide for those who have terminal or chronic illness. The Church strongly opposes these moves, rightly seeing them as a serious threat to the dignity and wellbeing of the sick and disabled, and to wider society itself.

The Church understands that grave psychological disturbances, anguish, or grave fear of hardship, suffering, or torture can lead people to contemplate suicide (*CCC*, 2282). However, suicide can never be justified as being in our best interests because it is an act contrary to love of self, love of our family and friends and ultimately, contrary to the love of the living God, who has entrusted the gift of life to us as stewards not owners.

If you find that your thoughts morbidly dwell on methods of suicide or making plans to carry it out, it's essential that you talk to someone you can trust, and your GP or nurse. In an emergency, contact the Samaritans. (See contacts on page 67)

Things that help

Hold a crucifix

There have been times when I've been in so much pain that I've been incapable of praying in the ordinary way. Pain can be so insistent and overwhelming that it is difficult to focus on anything else. At times like these I find I can't remember anything positive or hopeful.

However, I've got into the habit of holding a palm-sized crucifix or cross that helps me get through the worst of it. The shape and feel of the crucifix sends another signal that gets through the pain signals, and calls to mind, and heart, a host of powerful associations around Christ's love made visible on the Cross. More often than not, this gives me the patience and perseverance to endure, calming the feelings of hopelessness and desperation.

Furthermore, Jesus meant for the sign of his physical death on the Cross - the Crucifix - to become a symbol of healing, drawing the parallel between Moses' use of a bronze serpent to bring healing to the tribes of Israel and his being raised up on the Cross.

And just as Moses lifted up the serpent in the wilderness, so must the Son of Man be lifted up, that whoever believes in him may have eternal life. (John 3:15; cf. Numbers 21: 8).

Jesus' presence in the Blessed Sacrament

Pope Paul VI tells us that Jesus can be present in our lives in many ways - through prayer, acts of self-giving love, the gift of Faith, the guidance of the Holy Spirit, the Word of God, the teaching authority of the Church, and the sacraments. But above all these, Jesus' real presence in the Eucharist is the highest form of presence. (Paul VI, *Mysterium Fidei*, 35-39).

It is through the Eucharist that we come into the presence of Christ the physician, who brings healing to all who suffer. As the Catechism puts it:

Jesus has the power not only to heal, but also to forgive sins; he has come to heal the whole man, soul and body; he is the physician the sick have need of. His compassion toward all who suffer goes so far that he identifies himself with them: "I was sick and you visited me." (*CCC*, 1503)

One of the hardships of chronic illness is being unable to participate in the celebration of the Holy Sacrifice of the Mass, or Eucharistic adoration and Benediction. However, one of the most important things that helps cope with chronic suffering is being able to receive Holy Communion at home. After receiving Holy Communion, you can spend time in silent adoration in the Tabernacle of your own heart.

Also, you can pray before the Blessed Sacrament through online Eucharistic Adoration via a live stream at *www.savior.org*. This new form of ministry has been provided especially for the sick and housebound by the Holy Spirit Adoration Sisters of Philadelphia, Pennsylvania.

You can also participate in daily Mass through the live television programme provided by Mother Angelica's Eternal Word Television Network (EWTN). (For information go to *www.ewtn.com*)

Send a petition to Lourdes

The Marian shrine of Lourdes has been one of the most important places of healing in the world since Our Lady's apparitions to St Bernadette in the 19th century. Even if you are not well enough or otherwise able to physically visit, you can still place petitions to Our Lady via the Internet at *www.lourdes-france.org*. Your petition will then be passed on to a Chaplain of the Sanctuary who places them in the Grotto during the evening Mass.

You can also see a live video stream from the Grotto at *www.lourdes-radio.com*

Receive the sacrament of the sick

The Gospels show us that Jesus has a particular love for the sick, which he sees as one of the signs of the Kingdom of God. Furthermore, he commands the Church to 'Heal the sick' (*Matthew* 10:8) and personally instituted the sacrament of the anointing of the sick as the principal means to accomplish his will.

In the past it was the practice to only administer the sacrament of anointing to people at the point of death, but this has changed to include people who are gravely ill or before surgery, or to the elderly who are weak, though not dangerously ill (*The Rite of Anointing*). In the light of this, the case can be made for the anointing of those suffering chronic illness.

I have received the sacrament of the sick on occasions and have been graced with deep peacefulness and a sense of God's loving presence that I found healing. The anointing did not 'cure' the physical disease but it did have a powerful effect on the psychological and spiritual level, giving me the patience and courage to persevere.

Read the lives of the saints

When St Ignatius of Loyola, the founder of the Jesuits, was severely wounded during a battle, he spent months recovering from his injuries. This period of convalescence was to transform his life and the lives of thousands who have benefited from the charism of the Jesuits.

Incapacitated by his injuries, Ignatius spent hours reading books. Gradually, he began to notice that if he read tales of chivalry and romance he enjoyed merely the pleasure of a temporary escape that left him restless and discontented. However if instead, he read the lives of the saints and their struggles to imitate the life of Jesus, he was left with a long lasting feeling of peace, contentment and encouragement.

Reflecting on this distinction in his choice of reading, he concluded that God was calling him to abandon the romantic life of a soldier and embark on the more meaningful and fulfilling life of a religious single-mindedly seeking to follow Christ.

Likewise, I have found reading the lives of the saints, particularly 20th century martyrs, has provided me with the inspiration and example to make more of my life than suffering. I have discovered, like countless Christians before me, that the saints are invaluable channels of healing grace and intercessory prayer. The CTS series of Saints biographies is highly recommended.

Devotion to the wounds of Christ

Since the time of St Bernard and St Francis of Assisi Catholics have found consolation and strength from meditating on the Five Sacred Wounds of Christ - the wounds in His Sacred Hands, Feet and Side - for nothing better conveys the love of God for us than the Passion and death of Jesus. As Thomas à Kempis expresses it in his magisterial work on Catholic spirituality, *The Imitation of Christ*, 'Rest in Christ's Passion and live willingly in his holy wounds. You will gain marvelous strength and comfort in adversities.'

In particular, I have found meditating on the image of Jesus preserved on the Holy Shroud of Turin a powerful and moving way of joining my sufferings with his passion and death. As Pope Benedict puts it:

'Jesus is nailed to the Cross. The Shroud of Turin gives us an idea of the unbelievable cruelty of this procedure. Jesus does not drink the numbing gall offered to him: he deliberately takes upon himself all the pain of the Crucifixion... Let us look upon him at times of trial and tribulation, and realise that it is then that we are closest to God'. (Stations of the Cross).

Pray the Rosary

Another way of getting close to Jesus during periods of chronic suffering is through praying the Holy Rosary. Pope John Paul II expressed it well when he wrote that through praying the rosary we enter into Mary's living, eternal memories of the life of her son, and, as it were, see through her eyes the mysteries of Jesus. The Sorrowful Mysteries, in particular, enable us to join our sufferings with Jesus and Mary's sufferings:

'The sorrowful mysteries help the believer to relive the death of Jesus, to stand at the foot of the Cross beside Mary, to enter with her into the depths of God's love for man and to experience all its life-giving power'. (Pope John Paul II, *Rosarium Virginis Mariae*, 22).

For those who find praying the rosary difficult and for those who would like to deepen their reflection on any of the mysteries you may find my booklet useful, *Praying the Rosary with the Saints* (CTS D 664).

Questions to place before God

Why does God allow us to suffer?

'Who will separate us from the love of Christ? Will hardship, or distress, or persecution, or famine, or nakedness, or peril, or sword... No, in all these things we are more than conquerors through him who loved us. For I am convinced that neither death, nor life, nor angels, nor rulers, nor things present, nor things to come, nor powers, nor height, nor depth, nor anything else in all creation, will be able to separate us from the love of God in Christ Jesus our Lord'. (Romans 8:35, 37-39).

When I first became ill I had no problem accepting that sickness and disease are a normal part of being human. Our bodies are complex organisms to which any number of things can go wrong. I also had confidence that my doctors, with their medical knowledge and the modern array of medicines, tests and procedures, would soon be able to diagnose what was wrong with me and would be able get me well again.

However, as the years have gone by, and my doctors have not been able to cure me of my disease I have found it more and more difficult to resign myself to chronic suffering. In my distress and frustration I can't help asking these difficult questions, sometimes in anger, that believers put to God - Why do you allow me to suffer like this? Is it really your will that I spend the rest of my life in pain? If you are so good, why do you allow evil to exist?

Faced with these questions it is not uncommon for people to conclude in their anger and desperation that either an all-good God is not all-powerful and he has abandoned us to our suffering or else an all-powerful God is not all-good, and that he cruelly inflicts suffering on us. Having come to these understandable, but erroneous, conclusions it is not surprising that many suffering chronic illnesses or conditions decide to no longer believe in God.

However, Scripture and Tradition make it clear that God is both all-powerful and all-good, and also that he doesn't abandon people to their fate nor is he evil or the source of evil.

At first, in order to understand why God allows me to suffer chronic illness, I made the mistake of believing that God has chosen not to be all-powerful in order to create an evolving universe that is free to develop according to its own laws and powers. This includes the possibility of accidents, mistakes, and things going wrong, such as sickness and diseases.

However, I found this intellectual answer unsatisfactory the more I read the Bible. Though I still understand that God created an evolving universe, I came to the realisation, that if I wanted to be true to God's own revelation I had to accept that he is indeed the almighty, all-powerful God, and that he has not given up his power to intervene in his creation. As it states in Scripture:

'Our God is in the heavens; he does whatever he pleases'. (*Psalm* 115:3).

'And going a little farther, he threw himself on the ground and prayed that, if it were possible, the hour might pass from him. He said, "Abba, Father, for you all things are possible; remove this cup from me; yet, not what I want, but what you want."' (*Mark* 14:35-36).

This means that as God is all-powerful he could choose to cure me of my disease, and end my suffering and pain, but for some reason he chooses not to act. Having come to this realisation, I can either conclude that God is indifferent and cruel, or something else is going on that isn't easy to understand or explain.

After struggling with these questions, I think part of the answer is expressed in this saying from Paul Claudel, the Catholic poet and playwright, 'God did not come to bring an end to suffering nor even to explain it. He came to fill it with his presence'.

Jesus is this presence of God in our lives. As Claudel puts it, 'The Son of God did not come to destroy suffering, but to suffer with us. He did not come to destroy the cross, but to stretch out on it. He taught us the way to emerge from pain and the possibility of its transformation'.

It's true that the whole of the Bible, which contains God's complete and definitive word, does not present a theoretical explanation for the existence of evil. But instead, the whole sweep of God's saving initiative and actions presented in Scripture and Tradition are something better than a philosophical explanation: they are his loving, practical, response to evil. As Pope Benedict XVI puts it, God does not give an explanation, instead he acts.

God has gradually revealed his response to evil and suffering through the inter-play of his deeds and words through the history of his relationship with the people of Israel [Old Testament] and his relationship with the Church [New Testament] which is called 'Salvation History'. The *Catechism of the Catholic Church* explains Salvation History as follows:

'The whole history of salvation is identical with the history of the way and the means by which the one true God, Father, Son and Holy Spirit, reveals himself to men "and reconciles and unites with himself those who turn away from sin"'. (CCC, 234)

Salvation History is not some dry account of dead people in the remote past, but, because it involves the loving initiative of the eternal God, it is rather a living, present reality that we can enter now, through prayer, meditation on the Scriptures, receiving the sacraments, and devotions, such as devotion to the sacred wounds of Jesus and devotion to the most holy rosary.

Salvation History is God's response to our suffering, and he invites us to immerse ourselves in the healing power of his words and deeds through participating in the life of his Son, Jesus Christ. As the *Catechism* puts it:

'If God the Father almighty, the Creator of the ordered and good world, cares for all his creatures, why does evil exist? To this question, as pressing as it is unavoidable and as painful as it is mysterious, no quick answer will suffice. Only Christian faith as a whole constitutes the answer to this question: the goodness of creation, the drama of sin and the patient love of God who comes to meet man by his covenants, the redemptive Incarnation of his Son, his gift of the Spirit, his gathering of the Church, the power of the sacraments and his call to a blessed life to which free creatures are invited to consent in advance, but from which, by a terrible mystery, they can also turn away in advance. There is not a single aspect of the Christian message that is not in part an answer to the question of evil.' (CCC, 309).

Simply put, the whole of Christianity is God's answer to all our desperate questions about suffering and evil. It is an answer that necessarily touches all dimensions of our lives - intellectual, emotional, psychological, sensual, sexual, and moral. When we walk into a church, and most especially when we participate in the holy sacrifice of the Mass, we are 'inside' God's answer to suffering and evil.

Where is God in all this suffering?

At three o'clock Jesus cried out with a loud voice, "Eloi, Eloi, lama sabachthani?" which means, "My God, my God, why have you forsaken me?" Then Jesus, crying with a loud voice, said, "Father, into your hands I commend my spirit." (Mark 15:34; Luke 23:46).

One of the loneliest times can be during the night when you're unable to sleep due to pain, or some other symptom that causes sleep disturbance. In the solitude of the night, feeling in pain and unwell, it's very easy for doubts and fears to lead to anxiety and despair.

When this happens to me I try to pray. But often all the doubts start pressing in on me, due to tiredness and feeling low: where are you God? Why are you so silent? Do you really exist or are you just make-believe?

Some of the most insistent cries of the Old Testament, found particularly in the Psalms, are Israel's desperate questions: Where are you Lord? Have you abandoned us God? Why do hide your face? Often these questions are expressed in a very personal way, in reaction to illness and suffering.

'Lord, why do you stand afar off and hide yourself in times of distress?' (Psalm 9); 'How long, O Lord, will you forget me? How long will you hide your face? How long must I bear grief in my soul, this sorrow in my heart day and night?' (Psalm 12); 'I say to God, my rock: why have you forgotten me?' (Psalm 41). 'O God, listen to my prayer, do not hide from my pleading, attend to me and reply; with my cares, I cannot rest'. (Psalm 54).

Here we see Israel struggling with the reality of the hiddenness of God, which is particularly hard to bear during times of distress. But significantly, Israel came to understand that God is still active in his hiddenness, even though we cannot sense his presence or comprehend his purpose. Therefore, every psalm that questions God's silence and absence also goes on to affirm an unshakeable faith in the love and power of God, even though outward appearances may suggest otherwise.

Jesus is God's answer to our desperate questions. Through assuming a human nature God no longer stands apart and no longer hides his face. The Son of God became incarnate in order to make the hidden God visible to us during our suffering. As Jesus puts it, 'Whoever sees me sees him who sent me'. (*John* 12:45).

Having said this, it's fair to ask, 'If Jesus came to make the hidden God visible, where is He now? Hasn't he returned to the hiddenness of heaven, leaving us to our suffering?'

However, Pope St Leo the Great points us in the right direction in our search for Jesus, 'what was visible in our saviour has passed over into his sacraments'. (*CCC*, 1115). Where is God in all this suffering? He is present in His sacraments.

The truth of this struck home when I visited Dachau concentration camp as a young man on the feast of the beheading of St John the Baptist. In the grounds of the camp there is now a convent where there is perpetual adoration of the Blessed Sacrament. I learnt of the courage of Catholic priests and laymen imprisoned in Dachau who celebrated the Mass in secret in constant danger of discovery and immediate execution.

I learnt of the bravery of the Franciscan Friar and martyr, Blessed Titus Brandsma, whose only concern when being severely beaten by a camp guard was to protect the Blessed Sacrament he had concealed in his spectacle-case to bring to the other prisoners. Having succeeded in protecting the hidden host, Titus spent the night meditating on the scourging of Christ and praying the rosary, with the Blessed Eucharist held fast against his heart. On the following morning, he secretly gave communion to his comrades.

Jesus, present in the sacraments, brought consolation and hope in the midst of the worst depravity and inhumanity, he can do the same for you in your chronic suffering.

'There is no surer pledge or dearer sign of this great hope in the new heavens and new earth "in which righteousness dwells," than the Eucharist. Every time this mystery is celebrated, "the work of our redemption is carried on" and we "break the one bread that provides the medicine of immortality, the antidote for death, and the food that makes us live for ever in Jesus Christ." (St Ignatius of Antioch). (*CCC*, 1405)'.

Also, as Christians we bear sacramental grace within us like an untapped source of healing power - baptism, confirmation, maybe even marriage and/or holy orders. Each different sacrament makes present a distinct dimension of the Son of God's incarnate power and personality. They are here within you, waiting to become an active, living force in your life through prayer, confession and a life lived in Christ.

Why doesn't God answer my prayers and cure me?

We are afflicted in every way, but not crushed; perplexed, but not driven to despair; persecuted, but not forsaken; struck down, but not destroyed; always carrying in the body the death of Jesus, so that the life of Jesus may also be made visible in our bodies. (2 Corinthians 4:8-10).

I've lost count of the number of times I've prayed to God to cure me! Having lived with this chronic disease for so long I must admit that most of the time I no longer expect a miracle cure. However, when I suffer a bad relapse of the illness or some other disabling complication, I again, desperately plead for a miracle. But, as yet, God has not granted my prayer, or the prayers of my family and friends.

I strongly believe that God could cure me, because the Gospels are filled with accounts of Jesus' compassion towards suffering and his miraculous curing of the sick, but for some reason he chooses not to answer my prayers. Why doesn't he answer my prayer?

The Old Testament, which contains the Word of God, sees suffering as an evil which ought not to be, but throughout it recognises that all suffering, be it caused by nature, accident, human design, sin or Satan, remains within God's almighty power to avert or heal.

The Book of Job expresses the pain and scandal of God allowing the suffering of the innocent, while at the same time recognising it, in faith, as the mysterious working out of God's plan,

'I know that you are all-powerful: what you conceive, you can perform. I was the man who misrepresented your intentions with my ignorant words. You have told me about great works that I cannot understand, about marvels that are beyond me, of which I know nothing.' (Job 42:2-3)

So, having suffered for 22 years from a chronic illness and facing the prospect of spending the rest of my life coping with pain and feeling unwell I try to accept, in faith, that this is the working out of God's plan for my life. I've asked him to cure me, and he hasn't chosen to do so, therefore it must serve some mysterious purpose that I don't, at present, understand.

I must admit that there are times I'm angry with God for allowing me to suffer for the sake of his hidden purpose, and I wish he would at least give me a sign that it is doing some good.

Over the years I have come to see the wounds of Christ as that divine sign that gives meaning to my suffering. Christians down the centuries have seen a profound significance in the fact that after the Resurrection, Jesus' glorified body still bore the wounds of the crucifixion:

'When it was evening on that day, the first day of the week, and the doors of the house where the disciples had met were locked for fear of the Jews, Jesus came and stood among them and said, "Peace be with you." After he said this, he showed them his hands and his side. Then the disciples rejoiced when they saw the Lord.' (*John* 20:19-20; *cf.* 20:25-28).

St Ambrose writes that Jesus chose to 'bring to Heaven those wounds he bore for us, he refused to remove them, so that he might show God the Father the price of our freedom'. He further describes the Father embracing the wounded Jesus who bears the signs of our salvation.

Jesus' ascension to heaven bearing the wounds of his passion and crucifixion are a sign that he is taking up all suffering into the intimate life of the Most Holy Trinity. Our suffering is no longer outside God, apart from him in his creation, but has become God's suffering in the humanity of Jesus. I have come to see the wounds of Christ as God's promise that our sufferings - when joined to the sufferings of Jesus - have a meaning and purpose for the greater good - the salvation - of the world. And I have the hope, that when I die and stand before my Father he will show me how my suffering, joined with that of his Son, helped the unfolding of his mysterious plan.

How can anything good come out of my suffering?

'We know that all things work together for good for those who love God, who are called according to his purpose... What then are we to say about these things? If God is for us, who is against us? He who did not withhold his own Son, but gave him up for all of us, will he not with him also give us everything else'. (Romans 8:28, 31-32).

Often people suffering chronic illnesses or conditions feel that their lives are being wasted, due to disabling symptoms and being housebound. In the past I was haunted by the idea that men and women my own age were making a difference to the world, making it a better place through their work as doctors, counsellors or priests, while I was stuck in bed. These thoughts left me feeling useless.

Gradually I came to appreciate that though activity in the outside world was being denied me, there was work to do in the inner world of my heart. As the *Catechism* puts it:

'The heart is the dwelling-place where I am, where I live; according to the Semitic or Biblical expression, the heart is the place "to which I withdraw." The heart is our hidden centre, beyond the grasp of our reason and of others; only the Spirit of God can fathom the human heart and know it fully. The heart is the place of decision, deeper than our psychic drives. It is the place of truth, where we choose life or death. It is the place of encounter, because as images of God we live in relation: it is the place of covenant.' (CCC, 2563).

Chronic suffering faces each one of us with a choice - a choice of the heart - to either give up in despair under the daily grind of pain and sickness or to fight hard to find meaning and purpose in our suffering; to choose either life or death.

I came to realise that I was engaged in what masters of the spiritual life call 'spiritual combat' as I struggled to choose life over death. I became increasingly aware that there are spiritual influences in and around me, those that seek to oppress and corrupt me and those that draw me towards the freedom and holiness of Jesus Christ. As the *Catechism* expresses it:

'Prayer is a battle. Against whom? Against ourselves and against the wiles of the tempter who does all he can to turn man away from prayer, away from union with God'. (*CCC*, 2725).

For example, suffering can weaken our resolve to resist temptation, sinking us deeper and deeper into self-indulgent and self-centred sin. Or suffering can also strengthen our resolve to imitate the life of Christ through seeking to cultivate, through grace, his virtues. As St Paul puts it:

'We also boast in our sufferings, knowing that suffering produces endurance, and endurance produces character, and character produces hope, and hope does not disappoint us, because God's love has been poured into our hearts through the Holy Spirit that has been given to us.' (*Romans* 5:3-5).

So, one of the good things that has come out of my chronic illness is that it has woken me up to the spiritual warfare in which we are all engaged, whether we know it or not. And I choose, through the grace of God, to be on the side of Christ! (cf. Fr Vivian Boland OP, *Spiritual Warfare: Fighting the Good Fight*. CTS).

How do I offer up my suffering to God?

'I am now rejoicing in my sufferings for your sake, and in my flesh I am completing what is lacking in Christ's afflictions for the sake of his body, that is, the Church'. (Colossians 1:24).

Over the years I have come across advice that as a Christian I should 'offer up my suffering to God', but I must admit that for a long time I just didn't know what this meant or how to go about doing it!

Pain and feeling unwell isn't something I can get hold of and hold up to God. There are times when my symptoms are so overwhelming that I'm only aware of pain and sickness and all thought of God and prayer is totally forgotten.

The key to unlocking the secret of offering up our suffering is the Bible's understanding of sacrifice. The Old Testament shows us Israel offering God sacrifice - such as first fruits of the harvest - as a gift to God to express their love and faithfulness and also as a sign of their repentance for sin. Through these physical sacrifices Israel also experienced communion with God through which they became a holy priesthood and a people set apart for God.

It is sacrificial because the surrender of the first fruits of the harvest involves an act of renunciation on the part of the giver, to express gratitude and love for God.

However, as a consequence of the destruction of the Temple and the people's physical and psychological suffering in exile in Babylon, the prophets taught Israel that they could offer as a sacrifice their sufferings as a nation and as individuals. As Pope Benedict XVI explains the sufferings of Israel are seen as the true sacrifice, 'the great new form of worship', to serve as a 'spiritual equivalent of the missing Temple oblations'. (Joseph Ratzinger, *The Shape of the Liturgy*, p.45; cf. *God is near us*, p.34).

The Suffering Servant in the Book of Isaiah is the greatest Old Testament expression of Israel's growing understanding of suffering as the true sacrifice that expresses our faith and gratitude to God, and our atonement for personal sin and the sin of the world.

'He was despised and rejected by others; a man of suffering and acquainted with infirmity; and as one from whom others hide their faces he was despised, and we held him of no account... Yet it was the will of the Lord to crush him with pain. When you make his life an offering for sin, he shall see his offspring, and shall prolong his days; through him the will of the Lord shall prosper. Out of his anguish he shall see light; he shall find satisfaction through his knowledge. The righteous one, my servant, shall make many righteous, and he shall bear their iniquities.' (Isaiah 53:3, 10-11).

Jesus taught the apostles that Isaiah's prophecy of the Suffering Servant was the key to understanding the sacrificial meaning of his own suffering and death on the cross, which is re-presented during the Most Holy Sacrifice of the Mass.

As I have come to understand the sacrificial significance of the Mass I have deepened my devotion to the Eucharist as a way of offering up my suffering to God. When the priest says the words of consecration over the chalice, and raises it above the altar as an offering to God, and for our adoration, I pray that my sufferings be joined to the precious blood of Jesus in reparation for sin or for the conversion of family or friends who have left the practice of the faith.

At the moment that I hear the words of consecration I pray, 'Please accept my sufferings Lord for your intentions' or 'I offer my pain and illness for the conversion of N. (Name of the person or persons who have lapsed or have not been raised as Catholics). Sometimes it seems that my suffering becomes intertwined with the words of Jesus, ascending to heaven with the incense from the thurible:

'Take this, all of you, and drink from it: this is the cup of my blood, the blood of the new and everlasting covenant. It will be shed for you and for many so that sins may be forgiven. Do this in memory of me'. (Eucharistic prayers).

I must admit I often feel unworthy to join my sufferings with those of Our Lord's, but the Church encourages the sick to foster this devotion as an invaluable service for the good of the Church. Though at times it's difficult to see how anything good can come from my hidden suffering, I trust the Church's understanding that the prayers of the sick are an irreplaceable force for good in the world.

Pope John Paul II, reflecting on Colossians 1:24, explains that 'in the mystery of the Church as His Body, Christ has in a sense opened His own redemptive suffering to all human suffering'. (*On the Christian Meaning of Suffering*). It's not that Jesus' suffering is lacking or incomplete in saving us from sin, but rather that he enables us to have the dignity and purpose of being able to join our suffering to his suffering as true God and true man.

It is for this reason that devotion to the wounds of Christ is so powerful and transformative, because it enables those who are suffering to find meaning and purpose in the sufferings of God.

Prayers during times of suffering

Anima Christi

Soul of Christ, be my sanctification,
Body of Christ, be my salvation,
Blood of Christ, fill all my veins,
Water from the side of Christ, wash out my stains.
May Christ's Passion strengthen me,
O good Jesu, hear me.
In your wounds I fain would hide,
Never to be parted from your side.
Guard me when my foes assail me,
Call me when my life shall fail me.
Command me then to come to you.
That I for all eternity
With your saints may praise you. Amen.

Suffering

O Christ, my Lord, who for my sins did hang upon a tree
grant that your grace in me, poor wretch, may still
engrafted be.

Grant that your naked hanging there may kill in me
all pride, and care of wealth since you did then in such
poor state abide.

Grant that your crown of prickling thorns,
which you for me did wear, may make me willing for
your sake all shame and pain to bear.

Grant that your pierced hand,
which did of nothing all things frame, may move me to
lift up my hands and praise your name.

Grant that your wounded feet,
whose steps were perfect evermore, may learn my feet
to tread those paths which you have gone before.

Grant that your blessed grave,
wherein your body lay awhile, may bury all such vain
delights as may my mind defile.

Grant, Lord, that your ascending
then may lift my mind to you, that there my heart and
joy may rest, though here in flesh I be.
(*St Philip Howard*)

Christ's Passion

O Christ, I see your crown of thorns in every eye,
your bleeding, naked, wounded body in every soul;
your death lives in every memory;
your crucified person is embalmed in every affection;
your pierced feet are bathed in everyone's tears;
and it is my privilege to enter with you into every soul.
(*Thomas Traherne*)

Prayer before Christ Crucified

My Crucified Jesus,
I kiss the wounds in your Sacred Head,
with sorrow deep and true.
May every thought of mine today
be an act of love for You.

My Crucified Jesus,
I kiss the wounds in your Sacred Hands,
with sorrow deep and true.
May every touch of my hands today
be an act of love for You.

My Crucified Jesus,
I kiss the wounds in your Sacred Feet,
with sorrow deep and true.
May every step I take today
be an act of love for You.

My Crucified Jesus,
I kiss the wounds in your Sacred Shoulder,
with sorrow deep and true.
May every Cross I bear today
be an act of love for You.

My Crucified Jesus,
I kiss the wounds in your Sacred Heart,
with sorrow deep and true.
May every beat of my heart today
be an act of love for You.

Prayer before a Crucifix

Behold, O Kind and most sweet Jesus, before your face I humbly kneel, and with the most fervent desire of soul, I pray and beseech you to impress upon my heart lively sentiments of faith, hope and charity, true contrition for my sins and a firm purpose of amendment. With deep affection and grief of soul, I ponder within myself, mentally contemplating your five wounds, having before my eyes the words which David the Prophet spoke concerning you: "They have pierced my hands and my feet, they have numbered all my bones."

Litany of the Five Wounds

V. O God, come to my aid.
R. O Lord, make haste to help me.

V. Glory be to the Father, and to the Son, and to the Holy Spirit.
R. As it was in the beginning, is now, and ever shall be, world without end. Amen.

My loving Lord Jesus crucified, I join with your Mother Mary, and with all the angels and saints in heaven in adoring the sacred wound of your right Hand. I thank you for the boundless love through which you did bear pain so great and grievous, to atone for the sins which I have committed and now heartily detest. I ask of you that you

give to the Church and all her children strength to walk worthily in the way of your commandments.
Our Father. Hail Mary. Glory be.

My loving Lord Jesus crucified, I join with your Mother Mary, and with all the angels and saints in heaven in adoring the sacred wound of your left Hand. I ask of you grace for poor sinners and for the dying, especially for those of them who do not wish to be reconciled with you.
Our Father. Hail Mary. Glory be.

My loving Lord Jesus crucified, I join with your Mother Mary, and with all the angels and saints in heaven in adoring the sacred wound of your right Foot. I ask of you that holiness of life may flourish amongst the clergy and those who are dedicated to the service of God.
Our Father. Hail Mary. Glory be.

My loving Lord Jesus crucified, I join with your Mother Mary, and with all the angels and saints in heaven in adoring the sacred wound of your left Foot. I ask that you set free the souls in purgatory, those above all who in life had devotion to your five Wounds.
Our Father. Hail Mary. Glory be.

My loving Lord Jesus crucified, I join with your Mother Mary, and with all the angels and saints in heaven in adoring the sacred wound of your sacred Side. I ask that

you bless and hear the petitions of all who have asked me to pray for them.
Our Father. Hail Mary. Glory be.

Then repeat three times:
V. Virgin most sorrowful.
R. Pray for us.

O Jesus Crucified, add to these my prayers the merits of your Passion; grant me holiness of life, the grace of your sacraments when I die, and glory for ever. Amen.

To Christ's Wounds

O cheek of Christ, struck so harshly, teach us humility.

O sacred cords that bound the limbs destined to free us all.

O column to which Jesus was tied for flagellation, wash away our sins.

O lash that struck and wounded the tender body, placate those who offend us.

O sacred crown of Christ, grant us the gift of life and the rewards of Heaven.

O sacred Cross, beatified Cross, graced by the limbs of Christ, dispel all evil.

O you three nails that nailed Christ to the wood, pluck error from our minds.

The punctured veins permit us to support the suffering of the world.

And may the hammer that drove the nails, heal all
wounds, striking down perfidious sin.

Put an end to every wicked word, O mouth laved with a
sponge of vinegar.

Body of Christ, pierced by the lance, your love renders
harshness sweet.

And you, O body of Christ, set us free to partake of future
glory.

Most splendorous Jesus, Saviour of sinners, cleanse us
of crimes.

Mercy for the bitter passion, the flowing blood, the
sacred wounds.

Jesus is nailed to the Cross

What takes place now is so dreadful that one would fain
flee away, and not have to look upon it.

They nail him to the cross and then lift it erect.... O my
Lord and Saviour! But I have no right to make my escape;
I must stay here. It is for me he suffers.

On his way hither, Jesus has, at least, been able to walk,
to move, to exert himself. Now all that ceases. Now he
can do nothing more, only hang there in silence and
endure. The pain in his pierced members, in his head and
in all those deep wounds, increases and burns like fire;
more and more tormenting grows the thirst, heavier and
heavier the anguish and oppression of his heart. And he

cannot aid himself, cannot move, can do nothing, only endure and feel that he is on his way to death. And the multitude around! In his enemies, devilish hate and scorn! In the rabble, brutality!

O Lord, forgive me, a sinner! Mine is the blame for all your distress. And let your sufferings not be lost on me. Let its divine strength and patience become alive in me.

To every one the hour comes, when he can do nothing more, cannot shield his honour, cannot allay his pain, cannot find any way out of his misery. Above all it will be thus in his last illness, when he knows that he is on his way to the end, that the physician can effect nothing more.

Then each man is, as it were, nailed to the cross and cannot aid himself. Can do but one thing: recollect heart and will in God; hold himself firmly, unfalteringly, to the will of the Father and calmly endure to the end: leave it absolutely to him whether that to which he is drawing near be a peaceful or a bitter end.

Lord, when that hour comes, then you will be with me, that I know. The power of your cross then shall be in me, and make me strong.

(*Romano Guardini*)

Meditations on the Christian meaning of suffering

Suffering unites us with Christ

On the Cross Christ took upon himself the whole weight of evil and took away the 'sin of the world', of which illness is only a consequence. By his Passion and death on the cross Christ has given a new meaning to suffering: it can henceforth configure us to him and unite us with his redemptive Passion. (*Catechism of the Catholic Church*)

A sharer in Christ's sufferings

If one becomes a sharer in the sufferings of Christ, this happens because Christ has opened his suffering to man, because he himself in his redemptive suffering has become, in a certain sense, a sharer in all human sufferings. Man, discovering through faith the redemptive suffering of Christ, also discovers in it his own sufferings; he rediscovers them, through faith, enriched with a new content and new meaning. (*Pope John Paul II*)

God makes our suffering His suffering

As I beheld Him in His silent majesty hanging upon His Cross with the eyes of my soul, I saw in His gaze upon this world from His place of pain that there was no smallest trace of reproach, complaint, or blame, but only unutterable overwhelming love.

I saw that His love was our judgement; that as the eye must quail before the light of the sun because of the exceeding brightness of that light, so the soul must quail before His love because of the exceeding splendour of that love; and that that love was the greatest of all forces, the perfection of all power...

'I am God,' He said, ' Suffering is not natural to Me; as God I cannot suffer, but when I gave to certain of My creatures free wills and they admitted selfishness and sin into My universe, then of necessity there followed suffering, and suffering can only leave My universe when sin has departed from it. But when I saw My creatures suffering, I took upon Me a human nature that I might make their suffering My suffering. All the suffering of the world is My suffering; I have made it Mine in love; they that love Me may make My suffering theirs.' (*Father Andrew, SDC*)

God suffers with us

Christian faith has shown us that God - Truth and Love in person - desired to suffer for us and with us. Bernard of Clairvaux coined the marvellous expression: *Impassibilis est Deus, sed non incompassibilis* - God cannot suffer, but he can *suffer with*. Man is worth so much to God that he himself became man in order to *suffer with* man in an utterly real way - in flesh and blood - as is revealed to us in the account of Jesus' Passion. Hence in all human suffering we are joined by one who experiences and carries that suffering *with* us; hence *con-solatio* is present in all suffering, the consolation of God's compassionate love - and so the star of hope arises. (*Pope Benedict XVI*)

Offer up our sufferings

Those who share in the sufferings of Christ preserve in their own sufferings a very special particle of the infinite treasure of the world's Redemption, and can share this treasure with others. (*Pope John Paul II*)

Faith in sharing in the suffering of Christ brings with it the interior certainty that the suffering person "completes what is lacking in Christ's afflictions"; the certainty that in the spiritual dimension of the work of Redemption he is serving, like Christ, the salvation of his brothers and sisters. Therefore he is carrying out an irreplaceable service. (*Pope John Paul II*)

Faith makes suffering holy

The Christian must not only accept suffering: he must make it holy. Nothing so easily becomes unholy as suffering... Suffering is consecrated to God by faith - not by faith in suffering, but by faith in God... faith also knows that the mercy of God is given to those who seek Him in suffering, and that by His grace we can overcome evil with good. Suffering, then, becomes good by accident, by the good that it enables us to receive more abundantly from the mercy of God. It does not make us good by itself, but it enables us to make ourselves better than we are. Thus, what we consecrate to God in suffering is not our suffering, but our *selves*. (*Thomas Merton*)

The Cross helps us accept suffering

There is only one thing that enables us to accept real affliction, and that is the contemplation of Christ's Cross. There is nothing else. That one thing suffices. A mother, a wife, or a fiancée, if they know that the person they love is in distress, will want to help him and be with him, and if that is impossible they will at least seek to lessen their distance from him and lighten the heavy burden of impotent sympathy by suffering some equivalent distress. Whoever loves Christ and thinks of him on the Cross should feel a similar relief when gripped by affliction. (*Simone Weil*)

Our weakness joins us to the Cross

We can be thankful not only for the fragility itself but also for that more intimate weakness which connects it with the very centre of our being. For it is this weakness which makes possible, in certain conditions, the operation by which we are nailed to the very centre of the Cross. (*Simone Weil*)

Our anchor during pain

To deepen your spiritual life and fully utilise the suffering that God himself is now sending you, I will suggest the two following closer practices and self-examinations... it all aims solely at the depths of your heart and conscience, to help the fullest awakening and purification that God may call you to. Certain it is, that only such a growing, deepening (even if interiorly painful at first) can and will anchor your soul in a peace which not all the possible hurricanes of pain, or oppressions of physical weakness can break you away from, really, at all.

Pain - most real pain, which comes ready to our hand for turning into *right* pain - gets offered us by God. Try more and more *at the moment itself*, without any delay or evasion, without any form, as spontaneously as possible, to cry out to God, to Christ our Lord, in any way that comes most handy, and the more variously the better. 'Oh! Oh! This is real: oh! Deign to accept it, as a little real atonement for real sin!' 'Oh, help me to move on, from finding pain so real, to discovering sin to be far more real.' 'Oh, may this pang deepen me, may it help to make me real, real - really humble, really loving, really ready to live or die with my soul in thy hands.' ... The all-important point is, to make them *at the time and with the pain well mixed up into the prayer*.

How wonderful it is, is it not, that literally only Christianity has taught us the true peace and function of suffering... Christ came, and He did not really explain it; He did far more, He met it, willed it, transformed it, and He taught us how to do all this, or rather He Himself does it within us, if we do not hinder the all-healing hands. (*Baron Friedrich Von Hugel*)

The light of the Cross

The Christian is not asked to swoon in the shadow, but to climb in the light of the Cross. (*Teilhard de Chardin*)

The Way of the Cross is the Way of Light. (*Medieval Proverb*)

Christ is in suffering

It is he himself who acts at the heart of human sufferings through his Spirit of truth, through the consoling Spirit. It is he who transforms, in a certain sense, the very substance of the spiritual life, indicating for the person who suffers a place close to himself. It is he - as the interior Master and Guide - who reveals to the suffering brother and sister this wonderful interchange, situated at the very heart of the mystery of the Redemption. Suffering is, in itself, an experience of evil. But Christ has made suffering the firmest basis of the definitive good, namely the good of eternal salvation.

By his suffering on the Cross, Christ reached the very roots of evil, of sin and death. He conquered the author of evil, Satan, and his permanent rebellion against the Creator. To the suffering brother or sister Christ discloses and gradually reveals the horizons of the Kingdom of God: the horizons of a world converted to the Creator, of a world free from sin, a world being built on the saving power of love. And slowly but effectively, Christ leads into this world, into this Kingdom of the Father, suffering man, in a certain sense through the very heart of his suffering. For suffering cannot be transformed and changed by a grace from outside, but from within. And Christ through his own salvific suffering is very much present in every human suffering, and can act from within that suffering by the powers of his Spirit of truth, his consoling Spirit. (*Pope John Paul II*)

Meditations on the healing wounds of Christ

Every day of the week enter into one of the Wounds of the Saviour and remain in it with love. (*Saint Francis of Sales*)

Through his wounds you have been healed

This, in fact, is what you were called to do, because Christ suffered for you and left an example for you to follow the way he took. He had not done anything wrong, and there had been no perjury in his mouth. He was insulted and did not retaliate with insults; when he was tortured he made no threats but put his trust in the righteous judge. He was bearing our faults in his own body on the cross, so that we might die to our faults and live for holiness; through his wounds you have been healed. You had gone astray like sheep but now you have come back to the shepherd and guardian of your soul.' (1 *Peter* 2:19-24)

Wounded healer

Who suffers, and yet heals sufferings; who is smitten, and yet confers liberty on the world; who is pierced in the side and yet repairs the side of Adam. (*Hippolytus*)

Jesus allowed himself to be wounded

I adore the suffering King who feels my suffering; I love the sorrowing Lord who knows my sorrow... He allowed them to accuse him falsely, without opening his mouth; he let them drag him to the cross with no words of reproof; he watched quietly as they drove nails into his hands and feet.

He who created the universe, he who preserves the universe, he whom the sun and moon obey, he who rules the stars, forsook his mighty power. So he suffered with us who suffer much; he sorrowed with us who feel much sorrow. (*Anonymous*)

Jesus brought his wounds to heaven

We shall indeed rise again in the body. For an animal body is sown, a spiritual body rises: this will be more subtle, as the former is more gross, in that, so far it is compounded with the quality of earthly corruption. For how should this not be a body in which there still remain the marks of wounds, the vestiges of the scars which the Lord palpably shows? In which, not only is faith made firm, but devotion too is sharpened, since He chose to bring to Heaven those wounds He bore for us, he refused to remove them, so that He might show God the Father the price of our freedom. The Father places Him in this state at His right hand, embracing the trophy of our salvation: such are the Witnesses the crown of his scars has shown us there. (*St Ambrose*)

Christ's wounds give hope

My horizon - not death but Jesus resurrected, bearing the wounds of his crucifixion now reigning in heaven having endowed us with His Spirit. (*Donald Nicholl*)

The wounds of love

And therefore it is a certain thing, and good and gracious to will, meekly and fervently, to be fastened and united to our mother Holy Church, who is Christ Jesus. For the flood of mercy which is his dear blood and precious water is plentiful to make us fair and clean. The blessed wounds of our saviour are open and rejoice to heal us. The sweet gracious hands of our Mother are ready and diligent about us; for he in all this work exercises the true office of a kind nurse, who has nothing else to do but attend to the safety of her child. (*Julian of Norwich*)

Let go into the hands of God

O Jesus, will you one day put my poor soul and my poor life also into the hands of the Father? Put everything there, the burden of my life, and the burden of my sins, not on the scales of justice, but into the hands of the Father. Where should I flee, where should I seek refuge, if not at your side? For you are my brother in bitter moments, and you suffered for my sins. See, I come to you today. I kneel beneath your cross. I kiss the feet which follow me down the wandering path of my life constantly and silently, leaving bloody footprints behind.

I embrace your cross, Lord of eternal love, heart of all hearts, heart that was pierced, heart that is patient and unspeakably kind. Have mercy on me. Receive me into your love. And when I come to the end of my pilgrimage, when the day begins to decline and the shadows of death surround me, speak your last word at the end of my life also: ' Father, into your hands I commend his spirit.' O good Jesus. Amen ' (*Karl Rahner*)

The hands of God

'And I've come to think that the only, the supreme, prayer we can offer up, during these hours when the road before us is shrouded in darkness, is that of our master on the cross: '*In manus tuas commendo spiritum meum.*' [Into your hands I commend my spirit]. To the hands that broke and blessed and caressed, that were pierced... to the kindly and mighty hands that reach down to the very marrow of the soul - that mould and create - to the hands through which so great a love is transmitted - it is to these that it is good to surrender our soul, above all when we suffer or are afraid. And in so doing there is a great happiness and great merit. (*Teilhard de Chardin*)

Turn to Jesus in his pain

When a Christian believer is going through any distressing or disquieting experience, it can be a source of comfort and encouragement to him to remember that the Lord Jesus 'knows all about it, - that He Himself went through the very same experience. So when such a person is severely tempted he may be helped by the remembrance that Jesus also was tempted; and when he is let down or deserted by friends be may be consoled by the thought that this same thing happened to Jesus.

It is especially in the experience of acute physical pain that believers - and perhaps some who are not formally believers - find strength and courage in the thought that Jesus went through the same experience - in the thought of the nails and thorns and the pain that He must have experienced on the cross. History tells of Joan of Arc strengthened in the flames by the cross of plaited straw held before her eyes; and memory records a young man dying of cancer who, in the half-hour of agony when each injection of morphine was losing its effect, would slowly move his right hand across his body and cling to the Palm Cross tucked in his pyjama pocket. That Jesus went through pain is a continuing source of comfort and courage to pain-stricken people.

One might, when one is free from pain, raise questions about the logic of such comfort - about why it is that pain should be more bearable or more bravely borne for the knowledge that Jesus - or indeed any one else - has borne similar pain. But questions of logic do not arise for a person in acute pain: it is enough that he should find it good and strengthening to turn his thoughts to Jesus in His pain or to rest his eyes or fingers on a representation of the cross. (*WH Vanstone*)

The wounded God

The wounds that evil stamped upon the flesh of Christ are to be worshipped as holy not because they are wounds, but because they are *His* wounds. Nor would we worship them if He had merely died of them, without rising again. For Jesus is not merely someone who once loved men enough to die for them. He is a man whose human nature subsists in God, so that He is a divine person. His love for us is the infinite love of God, which is stronger than all evil and cannot be touched by death. (*Thomas Merton*).

Wounded love has a healing power

Jesus' wounds, in life and in death, are the expressions of his openness to our suffering. He suffered because of his love: his sufferings are the stigmata of his care for us and for the whole world estranged from God. Such wounded love has a healing power because it is enfleshed love, entering into human weakness, feeling our pain, standing beside us in our dereliction. (*Alastair Campbell*)

The power of Christ nailed to the Cross

Those who share in Christ's sufferings have before their eyes the Paschal Mystery of the Cross and Resurrection, in which Christ descends, in a first phase, to the ultimate limits of human weakness and impotence: indeed, he dies nailed to the Cross. But if at the same time in this weakness there is accomplished his lifting up, confirmed by the power of the Resurrection, then this means that the weaknesses of all human sufferings are capable of being infused with the same power of God manifested in Christ's Cross... to suffer means to become particularly susceptible, particularly open to the working of the salvific powers of God, offered to humanity in Christ. In him God has confirmed his desire to act especially through suffering, which is man's weakness and emptying of self, and he wishes to make his power known precisely in this weakness and emptying of self. (*Pope John Paul II*)

Love in the deepest darkness

The sheer physical horror of the mocking, flogging and crucifixion of Jesus takes us into the depths of human degradation and cruelty, yet in deepest darkness we find the flame of love. It is this intertwining of suffering and strength which allows Paul to see hope and healing coming directly from his own suffering... (*Alastair Campbell*)

Wounds are healed by his wounds

Thus by meditation and adoration people have drawn closer to the sufferings of Christ, participated in them and felt them as their own sufferings. And again, in their own sufferings, people have discovered a fellowship with the 'sacred head sore wounded.' ...The 'man of sorrows' spoke to those who were wasting away in pain, and to whom no one else spoke, because no one could help them... he brings help through his wounds and through what from the human point of view is his impotent suffering. 'When my heart is most fearful, help me out of my fears, through thy fear and pain,' says a hymn by Paul Gerhardt.

This mysticism of the passion has discovered a truth about Christ... suffering is overcome by suffering, and wounds are healed by wounds. For the suffering in suffering is the lack of love, and the wounds in wounds are the abandonment, and the powerlessness in pain is unbelief. And therefore the suffering of abandonment is overcome by the suffering of love, which is not afraid of what is sick and ugly, but accepts it and takes it to itself to heal it. Through his own abandonment by God, the crucified Christ brings God to those who feel abandoned by God. Through his suffering he brings salvation to those who suffer. Through his death he brings eternal life to those who are dying. (*Jurgan Moltmann*)

Acknowledgements

Dr J O'Donovan GP and Mr G Nasmyth, Consultant, for their help and care; Martina for her steadfast love and understandnig and all the people who pray for me.

Contacts

The Samaritans

UK: 08457 909 090

ROI: 1850 609 090

Email: jo@samaritans.org

Recommended reading

Fr Benedict Groeschel, CFR. *Arise from Darkness: What To Do When Life Doesn't Make Sense*. Ignatius Press, 1995 & *Tears of God: Persevering in the Face of Great Sorrow or Catastrophe*. Ignatius Press, 2009.

Healing Thoughts on the Trials of Sickness

Compassionate insights on sickness, and the care of the sick

These reflections on sickness and the state of those who are sick demonstrate Benedict XVI's great attentiveness to the meaning and extent of human suffering. The anguish of those in a worsening medical condition can truly be answered by confidence in God's boundless love. In the cross of sickness we suffer with Christ. Both the spirituality and moral dimensions of the care of the sick are also important themes. A booklet warmly commended to both the sick and those involved in their care.

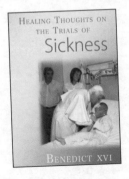

ISBN: 978 1 86082 720 4

Do844

Prayer in Sadness & Sorrow

The Healing Power of Lament

Prayer of lament is prayer in moments of deep suffering or hopelessness, when God can seem absent or distant. This booklet introduces this difficult but vital aspect of the spiritual battle. First the author considers the dangerous alternatives to crying out to God, then he shows how scripture, the teaching of the Church and the example of the saints can guide us in our journey from anguish towards peace.

The Deeper Christianity Series delves into the mysteries of Christianity, opening up the spiritual treasures of the Church.

Fr Taylerson is a parish priest in Trent Vale, Stoke-on-Trent in the archdiocese of Birmingham, and a tutor involved with formation of permanent deacons at Oscott College.

ISBN: 978 1 86082 778 5

CTS Code: SP35

Prayers for Grieving Parents
Spiritual and practical help
on the death of an unborn child

This book of prayers, practical advice, meditations and services has been written for parents whose child has died through miscarriage or stillbirth. It takes specific account of the particular needs of those who find themselves faced with the heartbreaking ordeal of such sudden grief, and will also be helpful for those ministering to them. It offers sound advice on dealing with grief, what practical steps can help, and articulates with great sensitivity the answers to the many burning questions of faith that such a loss can provoke. Together with prayers, and meditations on Christ's loss and vulnerability, this booklet is also unique in that it offers liturgies for the parents and unborn child.

Nick Donnelly is a permanent deacon and consultant on adult formation for the Diocese of Lancaster. He has been married since 1987. He has also advised on and authored several CTS publications.

ISBN: 978 1 86082 616 0

CTS Code: D713

A Little Book of Consolation
Treasured spiritual companion for those
recently bereaved

This thoughtful compilation of prayers, reflections,
hymns and scripture brings a great message of
Christian hope and consolation into the human and
spiritual void experienced by those recently bereaved.
Each chosen prayer and reading provides the sense of
divine love and mystery that lies at the heart of the
human encounter with grief and loss. The reader can
browse easily, in private reflection and prayer,
receiving Christ's consolation along a difficult and
often lonely journey.

ISBN: 978 1 86082 721 1

CTS Code: D739